MUSINGS OF MY MIND

Faith Maree

BookLeaf Publishing

India | USA | UK

Presentation by *BookLeaf Publishing*

Cover design by *Sunny Rewald*

Photography by *Anita Rewald*

Web: www.bookleafpub.com

E-mail: info@bookleafpub.com

ISBN: 9789358361438

First edition 2021

FOR ASHLEE

the man who jumped into the bathtub fully clothed just to put his arms around me when I was falling apart.

You show me every single day what real love looks like.

Thank you for believing in me.

A LETTER TO YOU

Dear Reader,

I'm at a point in my life where I feel like I've finished writing and reading over all of the chapters, and I can close the covers of this book and place it back on the shelf. I feel like I'm ready, like I can open up a new book with blank pages, and begin writing the next segment in my life series. I feel like I've finally come to terms with the life I've written so far, and what happened to me through those rough chapters.

I read that book over and over, probably a lot longer than I needed to, and I think looking over my past so much is what led me to write this literal book. I've realised that it's okay to read the same thing over and over, as long as you're learning something new each time, so I kept my eyes out for all of the things I missed, and oh, there were plenty of those.

I wrote this book for those who are still reading over their past chapters, looking for the things they missed, too. It's for those who feel their fire flickering out, and it's for those who wonder if anyone else understands.

It's time to read what you need to and then put the book down, so you can get busy writing the next one. There'll be so many things you find in the past, both the good and the bad, but remember that there is treasure hidden amongst the blank pages of your future, and I promise you that it's worth putting down the other books to find.

With Love,

Faith Maree

BE AN OPEN WINDOW

Be an open window for the breeze of inspiration to blow through, knocking about your curtains of sensibility as it feeds the flame of passion burning in your hearth.

YOU FOOLISH GIRL

I tried to hold on tight
But something didn't feel right
Always waiting by the phone
I'd be waiting past midnight

I know you said you'd call
And I said I'd never doubt you
But I'm having second thoughts
Guess I thought that you would come through

Never thought that I'd be played
Never even saw the game
I guess that's why I always stayed
You foolish girl

What was there to say
Since everybody loved you?
And now I understand
That confidence can hide truth

So I kept it to myself
Found a way to hide the pain away
Kept it all deep down
So I didn't ever have to break

Never thought that I'd get hurt
Never thought it would get worse
Through the pain I should have learned
You foolish girl

I see you now
Getting ready on your wedding day
You're with someone else
You've got a smile across your face

I wonder if she knows
All the awful things you did to me
I wonder if you're fine
Or if you have trouble in your sleep

I know I'll never know the truth
I know I'll never hear from you
No more "she'd leave if she knew"
You foolish girl

I'M HUNGRY

I'm hungry.

And not the kind of hunger that some chicken soup or even an
entire feast could satisfy.

It's a kind of hunger that's living deep within me, in my bones and
in my blood.

It's a yearning that twists my stomach in knots while it calls for me
to relinquish it.

I hear its call, but what can I say?

I feel its anguish, but how can I fill its need?

An empty jar I struggle to open for the gain of nothing, my hands
unable to produce a sliver of relief through their strain.

What can I do?

LA BONNARDIERE
49-MONTSOREAU C.
LA BONNARDIERE
49-MONTSOREAU C.
ELSTAR
LA BONNARDIERE
49-MONTSOREAU C.
LA BONNARDIERE
49-MONTS
LA BONNARDIERE
LA BONNA
49-MONTS

EQUIP ME FOR BATTLE

You want to see me beaten
Yet you give me what I need
Penetrate me with your lies and deceit
My blood has poison that will corrupt you
It will turn all you have against you
Pierce me again, I dare you
Watch your blood turn to tar
As my revenge tastes sweet but
Burns you from the inside out
And turns your heart to cold stone
Wound me and equip me for battle
You fool

KINDNESS COSTS

Kindness costs

Yesterday, I spent twenty minutes late, because I helped my
neighbour for five minutes more, causing me to get stuck behind a
truck on the highway

On Friday, I spent fifty dollars on drinks because if I only bought
the four-pack, there wouldn't be enough for my friends to drink too

Last month on my birthday, I spent my romantic birthday night
with my partner helping our family by running the weekly
Thursday night errand

Kindness cost me the last jar of sauce on the shelf at the grocery
store, because the elderly woman beside me was trying out her new
recipe and needed it

People say that kindness is free
Spread it like confetti
Like it's limitless
Like it's easy
Like there's not an inconvenience
But name me one person who gives limitless kindness and doesn't
pay a price

Kindness costs

HOW LUCKY AM I

Let me be your vessel.

Pour into me your finest wine and let me lay your drunkenness on those whose ears touch my lips.

Let me sing songs in languages unknown to man, let me unravel ribbons over the doorway of my home.

How lucky I am to be loved by you.

How lucky I am to be touched by you, to breathe in your fumes as you strike your match of passion against my chest.

STAY HOPEFUL

Stay hopeful for the sunrise
Stay hopeful for a ring
Stay hopeful through the winter
Stay hopeful for the spring
Stay hopeful for new people
Stay hopeful for new things
Stay hopeful for tomorrow
For whatever it may bring

Stay hopeful for a good meal
Stay hopeful for dessert
Stay hopeful when you're happy
Stay hopeful while you hurt
Stay hopeful planting new seeds
Stay hopeful in the dirt
Stay hopeful for tomorrow
For a person, for a word

Stay hopeful for a sunset
Stay hopeful for a friend
Stay hopeful for beginnings
Stay hopeful for each end
Stay hopeful for a coffee
Stay hopeful for weekends
Stay hopeful for tomorrow
For the breath of life again

SHOOTING STARS

Oh, how magical it is to watch a shooting star.

We watch, too busy embalmed in the glory of its light to realise its descent into nothingness.

Oh, how shooting stars are like people.

WHEN IT'S MY TIME TO LEAVE YOU

When it's my time to leave you, please don't let me die.

Don't let my smile be covered in earth, but instead wear it on your face when you remember how I'd smile at strangers who looked like they were having a bad day.

When it's my time to leave you, remember my hands. Remember how I would reach out and touch. How I would pour out all of my love through my hands unto whoever met my skin.

Please, don't let that part of me die.

People don't say it but they need as much love as they can get.

Remember my arms, when it's my time to leave you. Remember how they would open wide and embrace, hold tight and hold long.

Remember my words.

Don't let my rotting tongue cease to sing kindness and praises. Let me borrow your mouth so that I can bless it with the language of my tongue, that my light may pour from your lips unto those who walk in darkness.

When it's my time to leave you, don't forget my heart.

I know mine will stop beating, but remember how much it loved people. Remember how it would beat faster when someone else wore theirs on their sleeve. I always adored their vulnerability and courage.

When it's my time to leave you, wear my heart on your sleeve, so you won't forget how it would beat for you, too.

The day will come when my spirit is freed from its fading vessel, but know my words remain here, begging you to keep my spirit alive and close to you.

When it's my time to leave you, don't say goodbye.

Because when it's my time to leave you,

I won't,

if you let me stay.

LIVING MOSAIC

Sometimes,
when I'm struggling through life,
I imagine myself inside of a story, told by a writer;
a great creator who spins the tale of fate to my favour.
I think about sitting there on the floor,
in tears,
overcome by what life has thrown at me,
and hearing a small voice in the background saying something like,

"and as her heart poured out of her being, she collected it carefully
into a jar, closing the lid and holding it tightly to her chest. This
wasn't the first time she had fallen apart, and it wouldn't be the
last. But she knew, as long as she always had her jar handy, she
could catch her heart each time it broke, and she could put the
pieces back together again, just as they were before, all on her own.
See her, a mess on the floor; a beautiful, living mosaic."

SOMETIMES, BUT WHEN

If life was a journey from one place to another, and a relationship was plane transport to get there with the co-pilot you've chosen, I suppose you'd miss out on a lot of fun things on your journey if you spent all of your time bickering in the cockpit about which direction you're going.

Sometimes, we have complete control.

Sometimes, we have to trust our co-pilot, and let them take control.

Sometimes, when the journey is smooth, you can turn on auto-pilot for a while.

And sometimes, there can be a crisis that will need you both at the head of the plane and working together in harmony for the sake of keeping your relationship in the air.

I suppose the wisdom comes from knowing when the right time is for each one.

I KNEW I'D GROWN UP

I knew I'd grown up when the pouring rain arrived and instead of
looking for my gumboots,
I reached for my umbrella.

BODY SLEEPING, MIND AWAKE

Plenty hours of rest I've had, and plenty hours of sleep
But I'm still feeling tired and my body still feels weak
I hate that I still struggle while the others walk with ease
I use my energy to try keep up and people please
I don't know if they realise how much it costs sometimes
When social outings seem like mountains I'm unfit to climb
But if I don't, I'm left behind, if I do, I've overdone it
So either way I'm in my bed when flags fly at the summit
A constant battle between my body and overactive mind
I'm forced to slow my thinking down and age it like fine wine
I figure if my body's sleeping but my mind awake
I can make the most of my bad luck, at least for wisdoms sake
So here I am, I write these poems to heal my struggle and pain
In hope that maybe someone might read it and feel a little more
sane

I DON'T THINK THEY UNDERSTAND

I don't think they understand
The pain that comes with my loving
Each text left on read
Each word left unsaid

I don't think they understand
The cost to keep my love running
It costs all my strength
My arms kept at length

I don't think they understand
That sometimes it feels so lonely
Am I miss-able?
I'm invisible.

I don't think they understand
That I wish they'd get to know me
To feel their loving
To just feel something

Days and weeks and months and years
I give my heart on tap
Fill your glass up
Overflown cup
Drunk on my love

Then go on, go disappear
Because you've had enough
Drink me all day
Then turn your face
Glass thrown away

I don't think they understand
Love and pain
Go hand in hand

AUTUMN BREEZE

Autumn breeze sounds like autumn rain
Leaves on the roof sound like raindrops quietly clacking
Fools me into believing it's bringing me life when all it has to offer
is lies
Just like you

CREATING SOMETHING NEW

Sometimes I like to think that sitting alone in a coffee shop with my caramel latte and notepad and pen is something to be proud of. But it's people like you that crush the heart and soul of a passionate person.

You take my idealism and my "unrealistic goals" in your dirty, murderous hands and crush them as easily as you would a light bulb. Shattered fragments of my once imagination cut through the air before settling in a bed of dust where they belong.

What shall I do?

There is little point in recovering what is lost. I would only dive my hands into the earth, creating a dust storm that blinds my eyes.

And what is the outcome?

The very same hands that created the beauty I search for will be shredded by the remains of what you had stolen from me and destroyed.

How dare you.

How dare you take what used to give me life and use it to bring me pain. You scatter what I once loved to watch me search for it and be left with nothing but bloodied hands.

You are no man that attacks front on.

No, instead you take the things that someone holds most dear, and you use that as your weapon. And you are innocent. Did you use a blade and cut open my hands? You are smarter than that.

You didn't hurt me, did you?

You just stretch and bend and pull every situation until you find that you can hurt me by manipulating me to hurt myself instead.

You tricky, tricky man.

There I was, staring at my wounds with no success in ever recovering what I once had, and I have learned. I am unlike you.

Here – take my dreams and crush them.

Take my future and smash it into a million shards that fly through the air in a beautiful explosion.

Take my heart that loved you and turn it to poison so that it eats itself.

And then watch me carefully.

For as you take from me, I begin creating something new.

Never again will I dirty my hands as I fall into your trap.

Instead, I will use my clean, strong hands to continue to create every single dream you took from me, but create it bigger. I will thank you for stealing my future away from me, as I will make my future even better.

Take it all and watch as each time I become greater.

I become stronger.

I become powerful.

And soon enough, you will grow tired.

And you will grow sad.

Because soon enough, you will realise that whilst you were so busy trying to affect my life, you forgot to build one of your own.

SUN IN MY SKY

I have adored you all of my life.
When was it that you stopped seeing me?
When was it that my star was no longer a light in your sky, nor my
colours a decoration on your horizon at sunset?
When we were young, I'd only be found by your side, running in
the wind with our hair down, feet dirtied in mud and sand.
When did you grow up so fast?
I remember the nights we'd lay under the night sky, pointing at the
shooting stars.
I want to lay under the night sky with you, still.
When did you grow up so fast?
You've always been a sun in my sky, and though I know I'll never
reach you, I'll continue to stretch out my hands to feel your
warmth.

CRAZY

When we broke up, you told everyone I was crazy.

And yes, I was crazy.

Because there's only so many times a girl can be manipulated, lied to and cheated on before she starts to lose her mind.

TOO MUCH HAPPY HURTS

Too much happy hurts
Like cramps in the stomach when laughing too long
Like a body punished by too much sugar or fat
Like a staring contest with the sun and it's flames
Like a step in the shower when the weather is cold and your skin
burns like fire

Too much happy hurts
Like overdosed bodies in back alleyways
Like hangovers and come downs when the fun time wears off
Like a spoiled child with no kindness or decency
Like feet aching and covered in blisters after a night out dancing
with friends

Too much happy hurts
And we all pretend it doesn't
And we all keep pushing the limits anyway
Greedy for happiness, like it's a drug we're all addicted to
Am I addicted too?

EMPTY HANDS

Too soon was the time you left me
Too late was the time I knew
A whisper in the wind, I couldn't embrace you fully
Empty hands have I now
I thought I had you to myself and I thought it would be okay
Hold on tightly to something and see as all along you had
Empty, empty hands

I can't go back and change things
I can't go back in time
I sit in mourning at the memory of a better time
Empty hands have I now
And the seat next to me is vacant, where you'd once sit
I don't have the warmth of your body against mine, I have
Empty, empty hands

Too late to resuscitate, too late for me to heal
Broken pieces scattered on the floor as I stand in solidarity weeping
at the memories I'll never make

SCARS UPON MY SKIN

Feeling clever that you fooled me
Feeling clever that you won
You put trophies in your pool room
Before a race was won

You left me high and dry to date
And I just played your game
Scared of every wrong move made
I always bared the blame

Feeling done and feeling ready
I took my things and left
Nights spent working dead end jobs
While you held her in bed

Pushed past the pain, pushed past the lies
To try and build a life
Struggle street became the norm
While she became your wife

I never understood your game
Or any of the moves
Still I try to figure it out
As if I didn't lose

But if I'm honest, I'm hurting more
Because I can't let go
I held so close the weapons used
That made me feel alone

Entertaining the memories
I played them on repeat
My mind deciding what it wants
My heart denied to speak

And broken hearted just like then
I throw myself away
Like old receipts or worn out clothes
For time to take and fade

Why do I do this to myself?
Why do I hold on tight?
Why can't I choose to love myself
While I'm alone at night?

Why is it that I need his hands
To fix the wounds he caused?
Every time I have tried to heal
My mind puts me on pause

Why do I crave that tender touch
From hands that turned me blue
Why do I wish for closure now
When I'm with someone new?

Why do I wonder what could be?
I know I have it all
Perhaps there's still a part of me
That's waiting for the fall

The guilt builds larger in my chest
While questioning my mind
I'm trying to move forward
But I'm stuck here in rewind

It's like my brain just eats itself
And all thoughts turn to mush
My head becomes a slip and slide
And I don't know where's up

Everything feels the wrong way around
And I'm all out of place
Chaos burns behind all my walls
Not showing on my face

So when they ask if I'm okay
I say that I'm alright
But what I really want to say
Is please just hold me tight

I'm hurting and I'm lonely here
I always feel afraid
I hardly sleep, I hardly eat,
I struggle through each day

I wish that I could say the truth
To say how bad it hurts
But then I feel afraid that truth
Will only make things worse

I take a breath and take my time
To sit here with myself
I understand I'm broken
And I need to get some help

I wish that it was easier
I wish it wasn't hard
Wish I could make it through this
Without receiving scars

But scars are wounds that healed in time
So maybe I'll heal too
And they will be a memory
Of making myself new

Scars to wear upon my sleeve
Scars to tell a story
Scars to see I healed myself,
And know I did it for me

I think that's where I'm going wrong
I heal for someone else
And when the wound opens back up
I suddenly need help

Perhaps one day I'll have this down
I'll know just what to do
Until that day, I'll hold on tight
To scars, to love, to truth

And one day walking down the street
Someone might stop and say
How beautiful are all my scars
That I put on display

And in that moment I will know
I've healed the pain within
And I'll smile at that stranger
And the scars upon my skin.

www.ingramcontent.com/pod-product-compliance
Lightning Source LLC
LaVergne TN
LVHW051236200726
843510LV00011B/1585